KENSINGTON PALACE

I am sure that everyone who buys the

book will enjoy this unique collection of signed

photographs. All the royalties will go to

the Sharon Allen Leukaemia Trust.

HRH Princess Michael of Kent

WHEN WE WERE YOUNG

With a Foreword by Sebastian Coe

QUARTET BOOKS

The photographs of Shirley Temple Black, Harold Wilson and
Margaret Thatcher are reproduced by kind permission of The
Hulton Picture Company.
The photograph of Jeffrey Bernard is by Daniel Farson.

First published in Great Britain by Quartet Books Limited 1990
A member of the Namara Group
27/29 Goodge Street
London W1P 1FD

A catalogue record for this title is available from the British Library

Typeset by The Graphic Unit, London

Printed and bound in Great Britain by
The Camelot Press, Trowbridge, Wiltshire

The Sharon Allen Leukaemia Trust raises money to care for those who suffer

from leukaemia, one of the most distressing of all human illnesses, which is

also the single biggest killer of children, after road accidents.

It is sad and sometimes tragic that the need for such treatment and care

frequently cannot be met by the NHS and it is heartening to know of

voluntary organizations who attempt to address this need.

All royalties from the sale of this book will go to the Sharon Allen Leukaemia

Trust to help it continue and expand its important work.

As a vice patron of the trust, my thanks to everyone who contributes to its

future by buying this excellent book.

Sebastian Coe

Contents

EDNA AS A SWEET YOUNG THING

Gerald Scarfe

A gorgeous study of me as a teenager, by a once-famous artist — Dame Edna Everage.

Emma Thompson

Hayley Mills

Geoffrey Howe

Sir Geoffrey Howe

Lord Whitelaw

David Frost

NO
PARKING

Sue Lawley

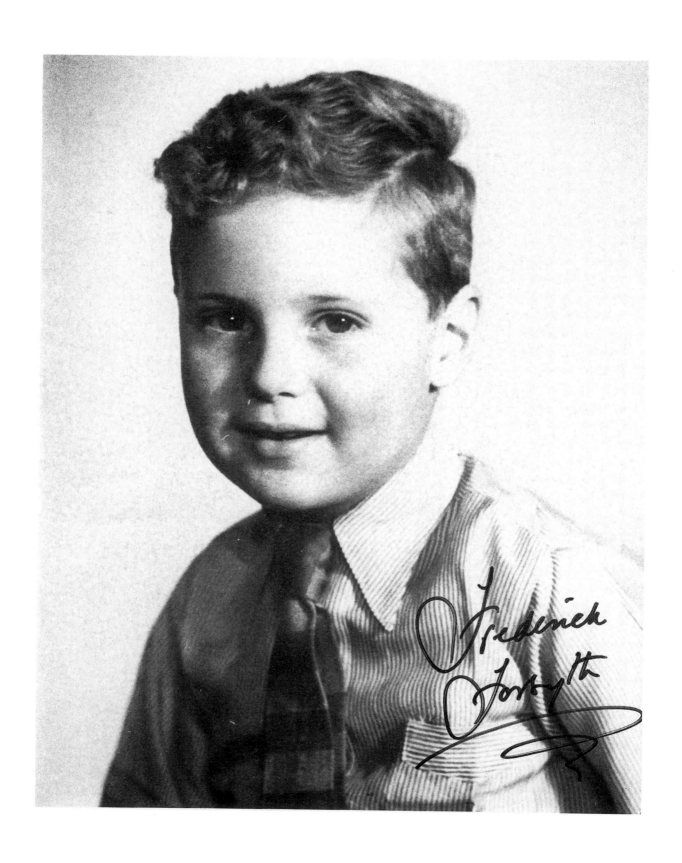

Frederick Forsyth

Jilly Cooper

9

Sebastian Coe

10

Sir Roger Bannister

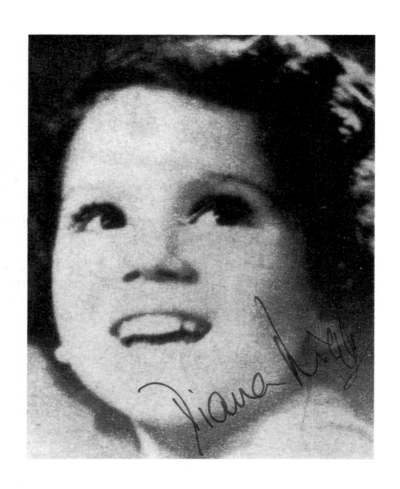

Diana Rigg

with love
from

Joanna
Lumley

Joanna Lumley

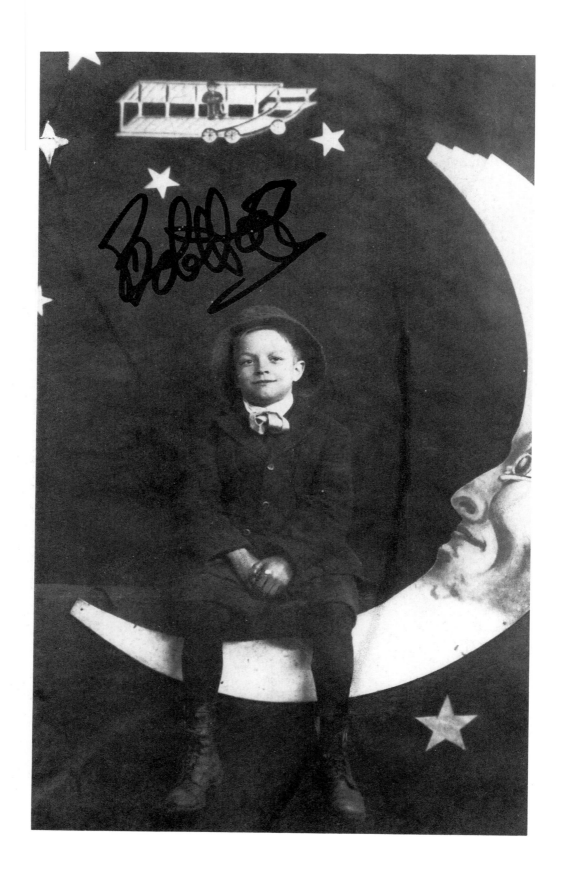

Bob Hope

Best wishes,
Shirley Temple Black
1990

Shirley Temple Black

Dame Beryl Grey

Princess Caroline of Monaco

Paul 'Gazza' Gascoigne

Stirling Moss

Cleo Laine

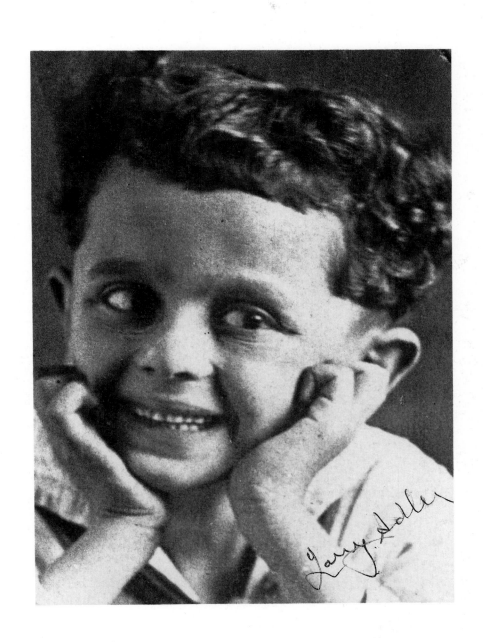

Larry Adler

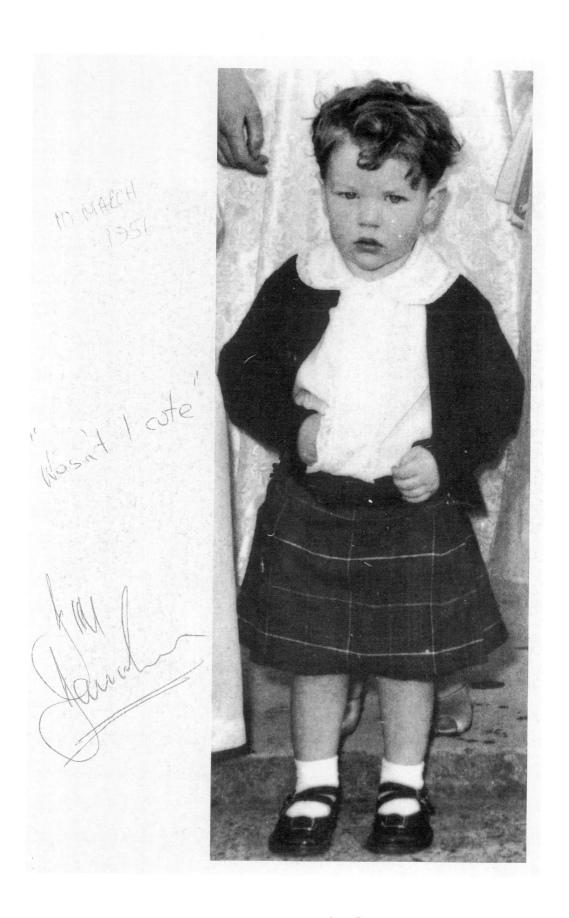

10 MARCH 1956

"Wasn't I cute"

Jim Davidson

Jim Davidson

22

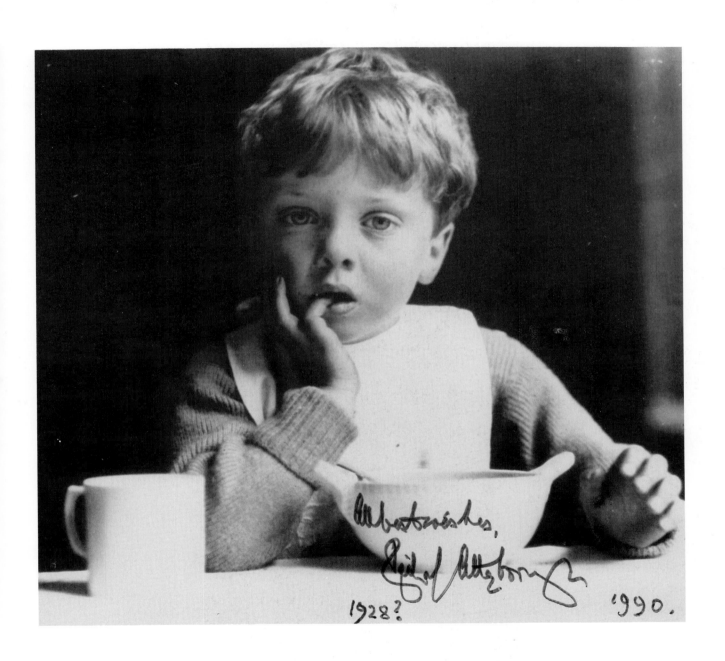

All best wishes,
Richard Attenborough
1928? '990.

Sir Richard Attenborough

23

Naim Attallah

1929

Bernard Weatherill

Rajiv Gandhi

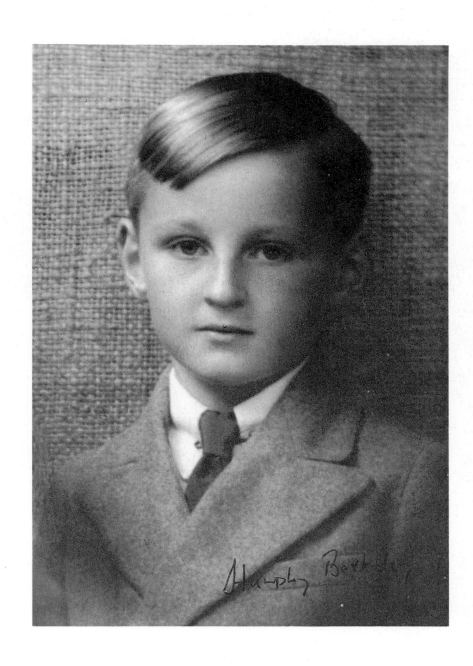

Humphry Berkeley

Anna Raeburn

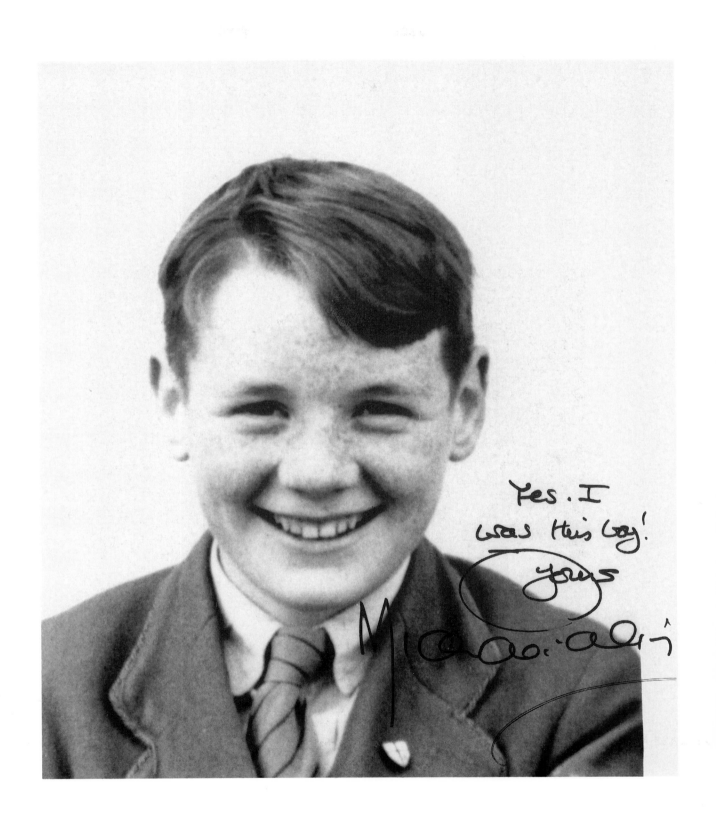

Yes. I
was this boy!
Yours
Michael Palin

Michael Palin

29

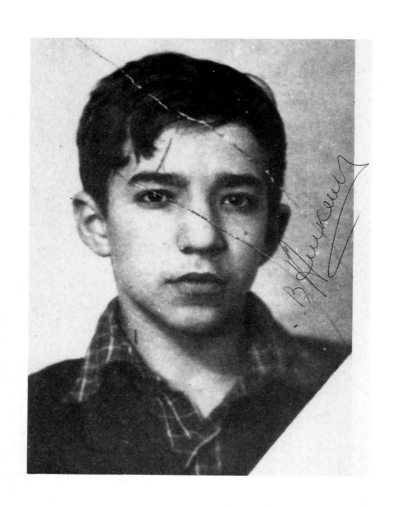

Vladimir Ashkenazy

Sir Yehudi Menuhin

31

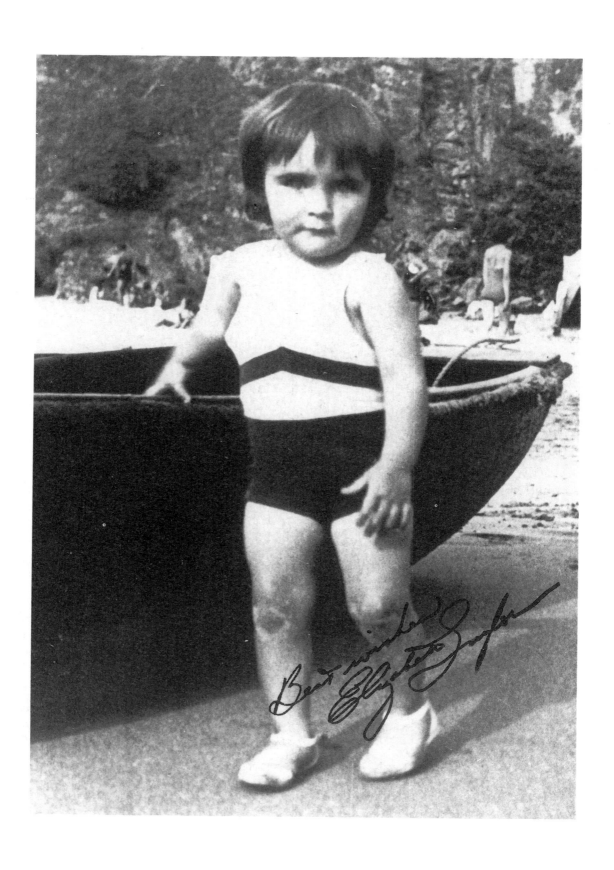

Elizabeth Taylor

Joan Rivers

Harold Wilson.

10 May. 1990

Harold Wilson

34

Edward Heath

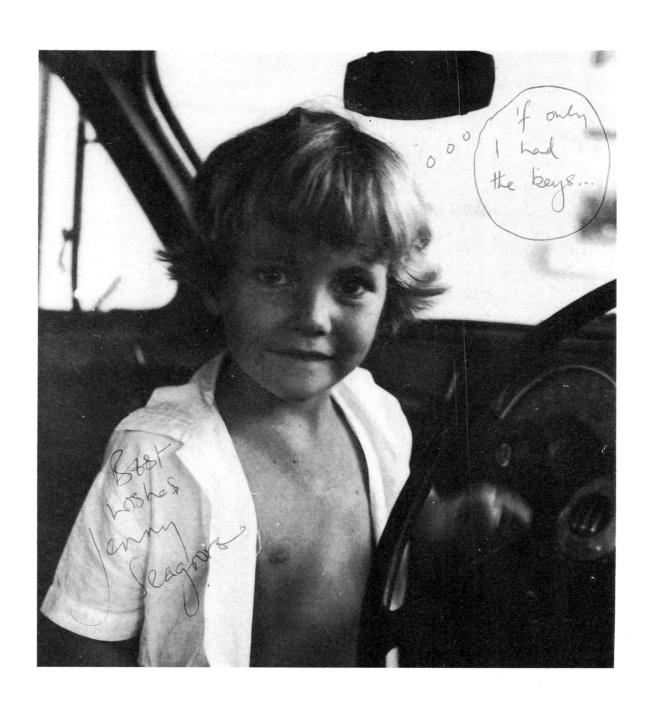

Jenny Seagrove

Michael Winner

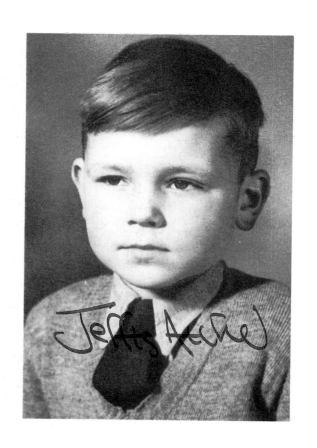

Jeffrey Archer

Barbara Cartland

Andrew & Julian Lloyd Webber

Dame Ninette de Valois

41

Lord Carrington

Quintin Hogg

Lord Hailsham

best wishes
Terry Jones
(45 years later and still
building castles)
Oct. 1990

Terry Jones

44

Ronnie Corbett

Ronnie Barker

45

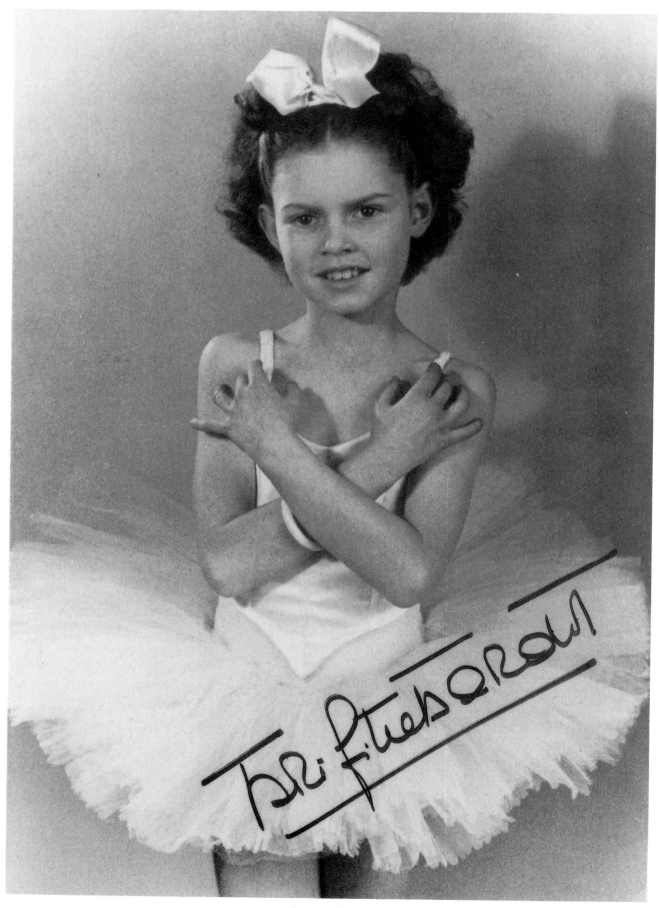

Brigitte Bardot

Deanna Durbin

47

James Callaghan

Lord Callaghan

48

Lord Rees-Mogg

49

John Cleese

John Mortimer

51

Butter wouldn't melt...

Maureen Lipman

Maureen Lipman

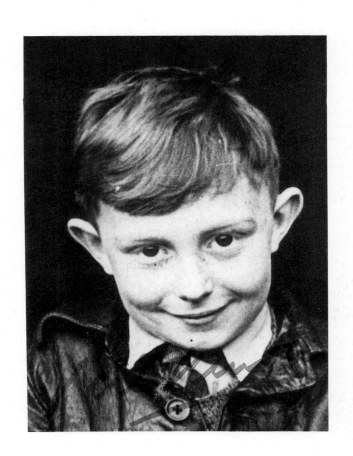

Neil Kinnock

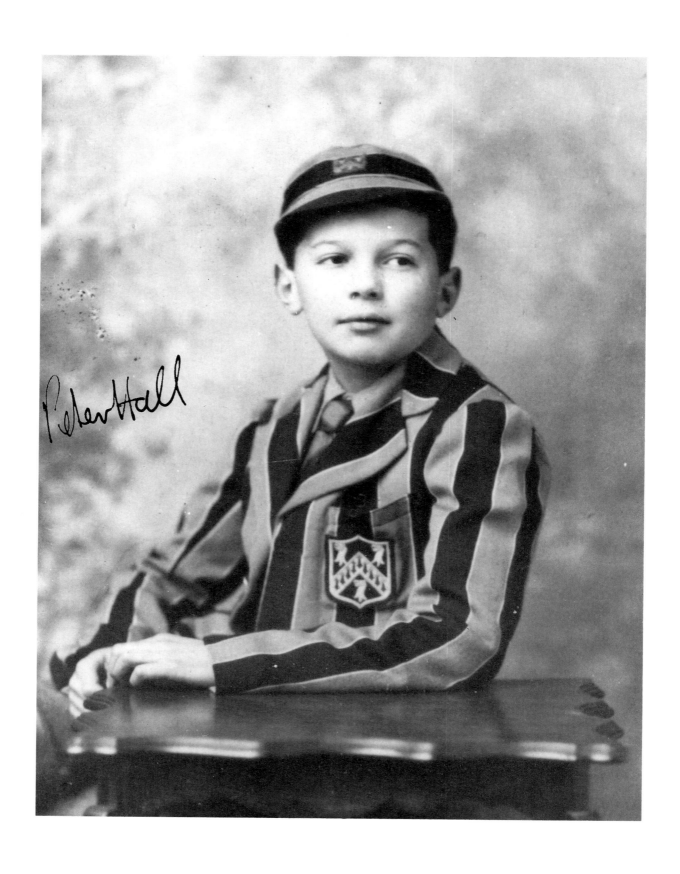

Sir Peter Hall

John Profumo

Valerie Hobson

Bruce Oldfield

Sir Hardy Amies

Margaret Thatcher

58

Ludovic Kennedy

Moira Shearer

Thankyou for helping & your generosity! A Very Young Roger Moore

Roger Moore

60

Larry Hagman

61

Denice Lewis

Lady Antonia Fraser

Robert Hawke

28. II. 1990

Chancellor Helmut Kohl

Auberon Waugh

66

Dominic Lawson

Richard Branson

68

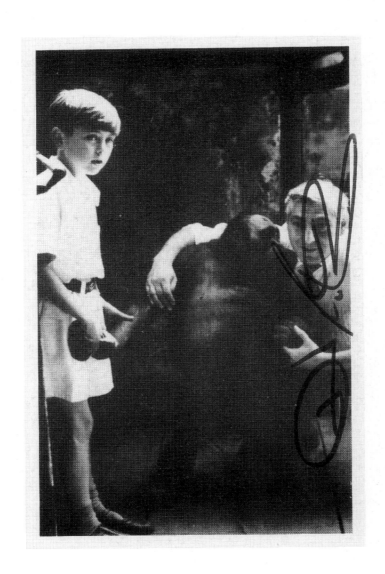

David Puttnam

69

Lord Home

Dr David Owen

Arthur Miller with his brother Kermit

Alan Ayckbourn

Albert & Michel Roux

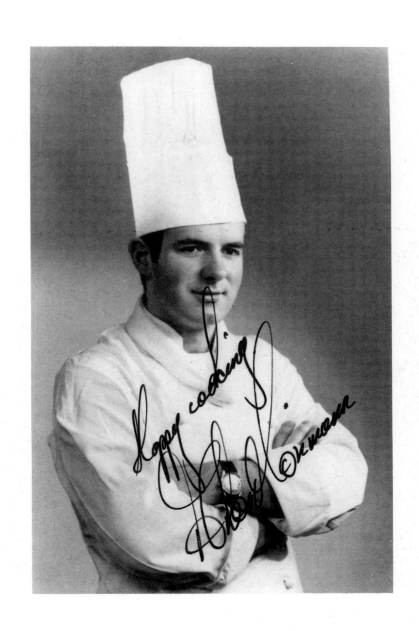

Anton Mosimann

Jeffrey Bernard

Joan Collins

My Best Wishes

Miss Bluebell

Miss Bluebell

Lord & Lady Longford

Yoko Ono

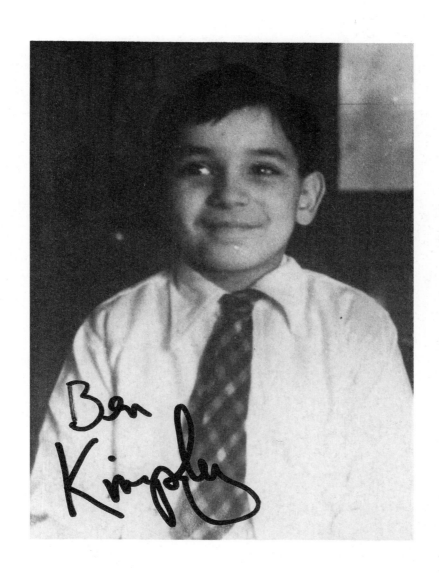

Ben Kingsley

Galina Panova

82

Cameron Mackintosh

with love
[signature]

Sophie Ward

84

Fiona Fullerton

Norman Tebbit

Dame Elisabeth Frink